What Wakes Us

Poems

E.K. Mortenson

Červená Barva Press
P.O. Box 440357
W. Somerville, MA 02144-3222

www.cervenabarvapress.com

Bookstore: www.thelostbookshelf.com

Cover Art: "El sueño de la razón produce monstruos"
by Francisco José de Goya

Cover Design: William J. Kelle

ISBN: 978-0-9910091-3-8

Library of Congress Control Number: 2013953561

Distributed by Small Press Distribution: www.spdbooks.org

ACKNOWLEDGMENTS

Many thanks to the editors of the following journals or anthologies in which these poems first appeared:

Beloved of the Earth: 150 Poems of Grief and Gratitude (Holy Cowl Press) "Cataloging Mistakes"; *Black & White* "Prayer" "Bystander" "Results May Vary" *Chantarelle's Notebook* "Long Slow Fade" "Reunion" "Saturday Afternoon" "Bigger Than A Breadbox"; *Connecticut Review* "Rented"; *hell stung and crooked* (Uphook Press) "After Shakespeare's Sonnet 138"; *Pisgah Review* "Tree of Knowledge"; *The Prose-Poem Project* "What Wakes Us—section III" "Diner" "Pre-Fab"; *RATTLE* "Dreaming of Emily Dickinson"; *Red Clay Review* "Ode to Trouble" "Sick Child"; *Six Sentences* "View of the Marketplace" "Winter Beach"; *The Centrifugal Eye* "Sleeping With the Seer"; *Third Wednesday* "One Day"; *Trillium Literary Journal* "What Wakes Us—section I"; *Two Bit Magazine* "Still Life" "Landscape #17"; *What's Nature Got to do with Me?: Staying Wildly Sane in a Mad World* (Native West Press) "Heartbroken"

TABLE OF CONTENTS

Then

Now

Later

For my family.

Worth waking up for.

What Wakes Us

I

Then

What Wakes Us

In the dream
                I am walking,
                just walking,
                                on a road, or in a field, or along
                                                the coast,
                                and someone
                                        approaches,
or is just
                                standing,
                                waiting
                for me,
and I am about to see
                                clearly
                                        who it is,
        but then

                        I
                                am
                        falling.
I might have
                stumbled
        on a stair,
or,
        perhaps,
                tipped
        slowly
off a bicycle.
I might have been
                                flying,
                                unaided,
                arms spread,
        and then dropped,
        suddenly remembering
gravity.

The dream
        ends
                abruptly.

So much so that I am
startled awake.

I have heard that   if you die

in your dream

                                     you die

            in real life,
so your body wakes you;   your time
                                     not yet come
I worry, then,

                          about my tripping on those
        stairs,

                     or falling
        off of that bike.
But I worry more

                              about that person
                on the road, waiting in the field, walking
                            toward me on the dock.

We can't always be sure
                    what wakes us,
                             early
                    or late;
                    what startles us

                                        from sleep,

                the small crimes
        returning
to our doors,
        reminding us
                of who we were,
        who we
are.
        Reminding us that

                                    our rest comes
                        with a price
                    that we are not quite ready
                                        to pay.

Quake

Outside my window,
                     a rustling,
the whispering
      of papery voices.
Outside,
                    a murmur,
                    a discontent,
                    an anxiety.

Little aspen,
      I watch you
                 quaking,
                      moved to restlessness
by a mid-September breeze—
          barely a breath, but enough
                        to set your teeth on
               edge,
                  to move you to
              chattering.
         Not enough to move the curtains,
                the air stands my hairs on end.
There is in me, too,
      a stirring of sap.

Little aspen,
      I know the quaking as well
as you:

         at too much life
                and the coming of Fall.
I also have felt that fear
         and trembled.

Prayer (after a fashion)

It's an unpleasant thing to bring people into the basic laws of physics.
                    —Steven Weinberg, Nobel physicist

I assume no position: no genuflection, head bowed or lifted,
                              hands clasped desperately,
nor legs spread, hands on the hood of the car or palms flat to the
                                                          wall,
eyes straight ahead. I assume no position, I do not assume: I stand
          and am—

                              what a little god am I!
There is no wish, no plea, no thanks in either my darkest hour or
          brightest moment:
all has occurred as I have willed,

                              it could not be otherwise.
          Subjective experience relates to physical process.
The forces that hold me to this world require neither thanks nor
praise, they require the acknowledgement of the mere:
"we work as you believe,

                              it can be no different."
          *Remember that everything you perceive, even this page, is being
                    reconstructed inside your head. It's happening to you right
                    now.*
I look and behold the grass, leaves moved by wind. I sweep my
                                                          hand
and buildings rise before where there were none.
          Without perception, there is in effect no reality.
                              I shut my eyes
and bring to a close all that was before me

                              —I am the ender
of worlds. I have numbered my days by the sweep of the seconds,
by the fly on my book rubbing its tiny hands,

                              by the torn paper towel just so.
          *Imagine that every moment and day endures in nature always. The
                    record does not go away.*

                              All eludes me,
all falls within my sight. This world revolves with me at its center,
a figment of my own imagination: including others, excluding
others

unawares.

Fashioning stone by stone, tree by tree,

        each day the world of my experience.

     The work of the observer is hopelessly entangled in that which he is

        attempting to observe.

I shall press pause freezing all where it is for inspection: dropping

     this one down elsewhere,

changing this one's costume, that one's character, adding scenery

               and lighting.

I have placed the chairs at the table,

     just so, simply

         by entering the room, engendering them

and their occupants, moving the past out of mind to be recalled

in the continuous present.

     There is neither time nor motion without life. Reality is not "there"

      waiting to be discovered.

          When I lay me down to sleep

            and die before I wake,

with me passes the world; with me mine, with you yours.

     The logic of quantum physics is inescapable. The trees and snow

      evaporate when we're sleeping.

When every eye grows dim, thus passes the world. Each day,

         fashioned in my image,

my boy rises, absorbing all there is—

       he smiles;

         he knows not what he does.

There, he drops bark from his upraised hands, here,

        pours water from a bowl,

   interrupts its flow.

     The universe bursts into existence from life, not the other way around

      as we have been taught. For each life there is a universe, its

      own universe.

Triumphant he turns, face glowing. Look what I can do, daddy,

        he commands

     with his smile.

   Look what I can do.

Italicized lines taken from "A New Theory of the Universe," by
Robert Lanza, in *The American Scholar,* Spring 2007.

Book of Days

These are the days
        when you most come to mind:
                late in October,
                late afternoon,
      the trees ablaze
        in russets,
        rusts,
        and browns.
Children play in piles of leaves,
    loosed,
      at last,
    from class,
their mothers
    at the head of the drive
      where they take
          one
    last
  look
into the mailbox.

There, for just a moment,
                the sun hits full
    and then,
it is
              November,
              with its gray mornings
      and its fog
        clinging to the pond
           down the hill
        from the farm,
      rolling through the swamp
          behind the pond,
          and across to the thin
        strip of land,
        sere
in these days,
            and over the corpse
      of the deer

hit by a car
but rolled

        somehow gently
under the guardrail,
and down,

these days,

       to the litter
nestled

       at the edge

          of the curb
and the road.

There, Then Not

When I remember
my grandfather's
      stonecutter hands,
          they are smooth
which is,
      of course,
          odd,
considering his business.
Of course, it may be that
they were not
          smooth
      at all
and the memory I have of them
              isn't, in fact, a memory
      at all,
              but what I believed them
          to be.
I do, for a fact,
         honest
         to God,
            remember
his eyes—blue, like mine,
         but not like mine
      at all,
                actually,
which are the blue
of the shallow end
         of the tropics,
the blue
of the continental shelf
         on a pull-out map
         from one of his National Geographics
            with which I would wallpaper my room.
His blue was pale—granite
         water taken up
         from the quarry in your hands.
There,
      then not.

Like his hands.
Like his business
        and his clients.
There,
        then not.
Simply smooth stone.

                        A memory
        for others,

                        but not a memory
        at all,

                                actually,
                something more,
                        something like a marker,
        like a dog-eared page,
        like a stone on the sea.

Bigger Than A Breadbox

This was the game
        I used to play
              with my mother:
                                one of us would tease,
                                    "I've gotten you
                                    a present."
                              The other, ask
                                    "Is it bigger
                                    than a breadbox?"

I can't remember
        how the game
                progressed
                        from there.
Besides, I was too young
        to remember
                breadboxes:
our bread came
        in a plastic sack
        from Angelo's
that we kept
        on the top
        of our refrigerator.

All these years
                later, sitting
        in this church,
                    staring
        at the hymnal
                in front of me,
        at the stations of the cross
                on the walls,
        at the stained glass
                twinkling
                above the altar,
I wished there was a way
I could wring the grief
                from your heart.

Wondering,
            if there was a God,

                                    before He received
the gift of your seven-year-old's coffin,

                                    would He ask
if it was
        bigger
                than a breadbox?

One Day

One day,

                                    you were gone.
But that's not the day
       that I remember:

I came behind you
           at the sink,
      your hands slick
               with soap and grease,
reached around,
      cupped your breasts
            in my hands and
      pressed my lips
            to the side of your neck.
I could feel your heart
      thrumming against the bones
              of your chest,
      flapping like a small,
            startled bird.

I don't know what day that was,
               but it was one day.

After Shakespeare's Sonnet 138

It took two nights
    of lying
          there
to notice you
        had stuck
those glow-in-the-dark stars
            on your ceiling.
On the third night,
      pushed
        to the edge
        of the bed,
I told myself
      you had arranged them
        in constellations
          that swirled
        and galaxies
      whose arms
          spiraled
      to hold me.
   Lying
      there,
I knew
   I was lying
to myself:
      you know nothing
        of celestial patterning,
        deep-space organization.
      You know only close-to-home,
          here-and-now,
      your own
         orbit.

Now, those stars
       shoot,
       lose
         their luster,
       fade.
The light they absorbed

dissipates.

Their shine
    a lie,

      reflected energy,
        fading

           into the enormous space
              of your ceiling:
           big enough

      now

        to lose
      those things I said

    to lie

here

           in the darkness

    and the lies
      you told

to keep me
    lying

here

        with you.

Split

what are the things
                    we
       split
when and if
                 we
       split?
do
                 we
       split
the house?
the cat?
the dog?
whose salary has to be
       split?
is that how they get 2.5 children?
by a
       split?
how can
                 we
       split
the shake of your hips
as you walk toward me
seducing
       asking
               wanting
                      givingtaking?
how can
                 we
       split
the flowers in the encyclopedia?
smile #377, the one I save for you
secondthing in the morning?
if and if
                 we
       split,

keep it.

        keep it
            all.

II

Now

What Wakes Us

In my dream I am dying, which seems to me odd, and filled
      to the brim with psychological meaning,
but now, when I think about it, I imagine it's because I couldn't
      bear thinking about the possibility of you
dying. So it's me. And it's strange, because in my dream we were
      sleeping, actually, you were sleeping,
while I was dying. No, it's not like what you might be thinking.
      You weren't indifferent
or in-the-dark, in my dream you were just tired. Bone-weary.
      And well you should have been.
In my dream, I was paralyzed from stroke or something
      of that nature (though I can tell you,
the mind is active even if the flesh is not so) and you cared for me:
      not like on T.V. where patients have dignity
and doctors and nurses care for that, as though dignity is enough
      to save us, but in reality: wiping drool,
changing dirty sheets, replacing catheters, heaving my lifeless mass
      to be washed, chewing my food for me
and spooning it between my slack lips. No small wonder you
      were tired. What was wonderful was that you slept
next to me in the dream, like all those years from then to this,
      while I laid awake and listened to your breath, in and out.
I woke up, not startled necessarily, just thinking, lying here, awake,
      listening to your breath, in and out,
relieved. Not because I'm not dying, but because I can't imagine
      you lying there in my place,
dying, and that I was the one bone-tired, breathing, in and out,
      asleep.

Sick Child
—for Anders

For the fifth time in as many hours I come to you when you are
        coughing, choking, crying.
This time I stumble when I see you standing upright, eyelashes
        glued together by mucus and tears,
grasping the bars of your crib, prisoner style, your tiny knuckles
        white even in the darkness.
You are too young to know how to be sick and the phlegm
        in your throat has steadily drowned you
awake; the throb in your skull has forced you into the only relief
        your animal brain
can conceive: you drive your head again and again into the bars
        of your crib, gasping for air
between sobs. I rush to you, pull you to my chest, promise you
        health I can not exactly deliver.
Upright, your throat clears, your breath returns ragged and wet
        past your submerged
thumb. Even in the blue glow of the clock I can see the fever flush
        along your jaw and neck
as you wrap your arms around me, burying your face in my
        shoulder, sticky with spit and snot.
Your eyes roll and you hover between this world and the other.
        Slowly, you give over as we rock.
We will not, I know, hold each other like this for much longer:
        the spider silk of your hair, crazed
from thrashing, tickles my face but I don't move, terrified
        to wake you, to spill the overfull cup of your sleep.

Rented

My neighbor, in apartment 13-H, has moved in to die. I see her,
       every day, as I drive up the drive, just a flash,
or more, perhaps, as her window, full-length, is directly across from
       the speed bump that slows my progress home
or away, the hesitation I must make in the face of death. She sits in
       a wheelchair, housecoat-clad, with a tray by her side.
It's odd, I think, to see the furniture in her apartment since she
       only needs one piece: her moveable seat.
Hers is the only basement apartment, built into the side of the hill.
       Turnover is high: no light, I suspect, front door and
only window next to each other. She's already moved
       underground: taking a trial run, getting used to the earth.
I wonder today, as I slow in passing, if she's given the nurse certain
       instructions: turn down the heat a little
more each day, draw the blinds and keep them closed starting
       tomorrow: make light seep in, trickle, struggle,
until the effort weighs down my eyes; until the dark is easier.

Cataloging Mistakes

and then there was the time her father died and she asked me
        where I thought souls go afterwards and I said
why do they have to go anywhere maybe they die too and are
        finally at peace and what makes you
think we have a soul anyway maybe when we die we die and
        that's it and that's all and sometimes dead is better
and wasn't that true for him and then she just cried harder than
        before but quieter and I knew she would
the whole time I was saying this but I couldn't stop myself I don't
        know what made me think that would be helpful
that it would actually be a comfort to her I just couldn't say
        what she wanted like that souls
go to heaven and watch over us but even worse was what I never
        thought to say at all which was that his soul
was in the way she held her chin just there and in the curls
        of her hair and the gold flecks in the blue of her eyes
and in her mouth when she peeled cut and ate a pear with a slim
        knife and her thumb and that his soul was in her heart
when she asked me the question in the first place

Dreaming of Emily Dickinson

I did again last night and when I told my wife she said,
"Are you, like, in *love* with her or something?" And I remembered a
            letter that Thomas Wentworth Higginson wrote to
      his wife—he was a writer for the *Atlantic Monthly* to whom

            Emily would send her poems for comment—
      about the time he went to visit her and she talked so much
and so fast that he wrote that he was glad that they didn't live

            next door to her, if you know what I mean.
But then again, he wrote to that same wife when he was a colonel
            of, of all things, an all-black, South Carolinian,
Civil War regiment, that he didn't see what all the fuss was about

            now that he was there, since it seemed clear
      that slaves didn't mind being slaves since he rode by
on his horse and saw a group of them singing.

            No one sings who is unhappy. Her selection of old
Tommy Boy as a reader of her work is the only intellectual failing
            I permanently charge Emily with.
      So, no, dear, I am not "in love with her

            or something," because if that clown didn't want
      to live *next door* to her, I would never want to live *with* her.
But I would like to visit her for tea.

            She'd brew it herself because they wouldn't have bags
and it would taste unusual and her house would smell like
            shortbread and fresh ferns
      and she'd talk and talk and move through the house

            like a bird and I'd try to ask questions like where
      those metaphors of hers *come* from
and, seriously, I won't tell anyone, but what's the deal

            with the dash and the capital letters? Do you, as I
sometimes—like Every three Years Or so—

have to admit, in the absence of contrary
evidence, just not get it? Not care?

Do you compose in your head hearing so much of
your hymnal that your rhythms are natural, like the way
someone said that Shakespeare thought in iambic pentameter?

Or when the Second Great Awakening popped its tents
on the Amherst town green, did you garden instead of get saved?
But I never got a word in edgewise
because she was busy with narrow fellows

and broken planks and frogs and flies and chariots
and loaded guns and sifting sugar on the shortbread
from a leaden sieve. Finally I broke in and asked,

"Now Em, I know that your business is circumference,
and that's all fine and good, though no one I know *gets that*,
but, um, do you ever let your hair down?
I mean literally. Out of that bun?"

For the first time she is struck dumb,
mouth slack. I rise from the small tea table
in the parlor and approach her carefully.

When I extend my hands past her head
she gasps shortly and closes her eyes as I pull the pins
from her hair. It falls long and lustrous
and auburn and I run my fingers through it,

pulling it straight,
keeping the top of her head
from coming off.

Ode to Trouble

When you look for it, you find it, a woman I once lived with
    used to say, but that is not always the case as you well know:
sometimes Trouble finds you. Like when it walks in on ballet flats
    or sling backs or mules or just flip-flops peeking little painted
jewel toenails or one inch heels or two inch or three inch, but
    five inches or more and Trouble charges an hourly rate
or at least twenty to sit on your lap. Or when Trouble wears a
    business suit and dares you to wonder what's underneath
or a bouncy skirt and dares you to wonder if *anything*
    is underneath or flirty low-rise jeans so that when Trouble
bends over you don't *have* to wonder. Sometimes Trouble stands
    so close on the subway or in the elevator you can smell
its soap, and the sweat trickles down your back. But you weren't
    looking for Trouble at all—honest—but you were looking *at* it,
especially the space between the waist of those flirty low-rise jeans
    and the high hem of the shirt that shows just the bottom
of Trouble's tattoo on the bottom of Trouble's back, and when
    you look up into the mirror at the end of the bar you see that
Trouble has eased onto the stool next to yours so you start
    tapping your glass with your ring:

dot dot dot dash dash dash dot dot dot.

Aubade

The radio broke yesterday and we were stunned. All was lost, and so early in the morning. What would we discuss? We had the newspaper of course,

but the silence. The silence could kill. That voice had come to us in the morning while you sectioned grapefruit. You were the only person I ever knew

who peeled and ate grapefruit like an orange. Who does that, I had wondered. Your fingers separating flesh from rind, delicately stripping off pith

and its clingy bitterness. Why, I asked, do you do that? You didn't look up but continued the grapefruit peel, Because I don't see the need to dirty a spoon

and bowl first thing in the morning and these come in their own wrapper. Why, I wonder, don't people eat grapefruits this way? Who decided grapefruits

earned the dignity of utensils but oranges didn't? Is it size? Does bigger deserve more dignity, force etiquette? I had to lay the newspaper down to consider that.

There was no mention of this phenomenon in the *Times* that morning. Not in the Metro section nor the National nor the Arts and Leisure. Clearly, this was

not a leisure activity. This was serious. This wouldn't have been on the radio, I felt sure. Surely, at ten to the hour there would be no report on the sectioning

of grapefruit, or an exposé on the "peeling counterculture." No emergency broadcast tone would be followed by a breathless, anxious report announcing the brutal civil grapefruit war raging in the nation's households, threatening to erupt across the globe. Traffic and weather together didn't seem affected on the 6's or the 8's

or the 10's no matter how many sections there were. There was nothing but static between the peelers and the cutter-spooners. I picked up the paper again

and asked you when you thought you might be able to get a new radio. Why? Is it broken? I hadn't even noticed, you said.

Saturday Afternoon

Across my fence, my neighbors sit on their porch. Four young
        men, early or mid twenties,
enjoying a few cold ones, deriding me and mine under their breath,
        and chatting about their plans
for the evening, no doubt: where they plan to continue their beer
        drinking, or whether to switch to cocktails
to impress the ladies, debating where the hotter hotties would be.
        One of them might
be in the discussion, or not; he has a steady girlfriend—the only
        woman I ever see at the house.
I've even said hello to her once or twice as I chase my son around
        the yard. Remember that?
one of my father-friends asks, as we push our kids higher on the
        swings after my neighbors let out
primal guffaws—some joke, no doubt, about the prowess one of
        them possesses in (choose one:) sports/drink/women.
Yes, I do, I answer. I miss that, he confides to me. Really? I
        wonder. There they sit, out of place
in this family neighborhood, four guys renting a single-family,
        center-hall colonial frat house. Truth be told,
they make little noise given their leased Hummers and Beemers.
        There are no all-hours comings and goings,
no strange women slipping away early on a Sunday morning as I
        gather the paper. Right now, it is us:
thirtysomethings clutching our heavily fortified sangrias in crystal
        stemware, our kids tearing back and forth
across the yard, screaming to be heard, who drive my neighbors
        indoors. They curse us, I imagine:
why don't they be a little more considerate? Yeah, it's a little
        selfish, don't you think? They should control
those kids. Indoors, they scoff at our trapped suburban lives while
        Guitar Hero boots up. Higher, daddy, higher,
my son begs, head thrown back, hair streaming. I close my eyes,
        inhale deeply, smell that fresh prison air.

Hood

She was just dying to say something, my wife,
        the whole time,
but we simply could *not* outpace her—the woman
        in the celery raincoat.
I thought I knew what she wanted to say, my wife:
        "That's, um, quite a look
you have going on there": leopard print dress,
        made of a spandex blend
that accentuated every curve, purple scarf tossed particularly
        haphazardly around her neck,
large gold belt—at least 18 inches wide—helping to create an
        hourglass effect, and gold lameé
shoes—from what I could see, a half-size too small and worn
        through the toe.
She kept pace with us the entire time, bobbing to the jangle
        of her outlandish gold
hoop earrings and the bangles on her wrists: a tribal throwback
        to a world far from here.
When she finally stopped to smell the flowers—no shit—at a
        bodega on the corner of 78th Street,
we were at last able to gain some distance. "Did you see that?"
        my wife asked. "See what?"
I joked. I waited for the fashion critique, but instead:
        "Did you see what
she was holding?" "Well, yeah," I answered. "A cup of yogurt."
        "Girl's gotta eat, too.
Maybe it was her 'lunch break'." "But it was *lite* yogurt,"
        my wife said. Then:
"What was she even doing down here?" I'll confess that question
        had occurred to me as well:
What, exactly, was a 225-pound hooker doing in our Upper East
        Side neighborhood, at 9.30 at night,
carrying a container of lite yogurt? Had she just come from, ahem,
        work, the way I might
walk through her neighborhood after an evening at Columbia?
        She, no doubt, felt
the same way I did. Or no, not the same at all: she in her sleek
        skin tight dress, revealing far too much flesh

compared to me in my flannels and khakis. Did I remember her
        cinching the belt of her raincoat
that much tighter? No. She flaunted more, hoping to stun us
        into leaving her alone.
Truth be told, I think we white folks around here are far more
        terrifying—we aren't loud, we don't joke,
don't whistle or flirt playfully. Content, instead, to judge, to pierce,
        to force you to wonder
what our awful silence, our wounding disdain could mean. I
        stopped abruptly and my wife asked,
"What are you doing?" "Just smelling these flowers," I said.

The Museum of Envy

Past all of the far more popular and corporately sponsored exhibits,
   in the sub-basement
beneath the snackbar, is the Poetry Room, where, under glass,
   in humidity controlled stasis,
untouchable as ever, lie the works of those daughters- and sons-of-
   bitches: Dickinsons and Frosts
and Kirbys and Williamses—W.C. and C.K. both—and every
   award-winning, tenure approved,
grant-recipient of a poet in North America. There are, of course,
   students sitting on the floor, diligently copying
verse from the masters, hoping to catch a whisper of tone, a
   glimpse of the elegiac, a whiff of organic form.
Do they? I think not. I wouldn't catch myself dead genuflecting
   in front of the cases,
sitting in cross-legged mockery of the Buddha, hoping against hope
   that in some life—this one or the next—
my work would one day appear under glass, preserved for
   posterity. I pause and take in the whole
thinking not of a great robbery, replete with diversionary smoke,
   helicopters, shootouts, and a miraculous escape
resulting in a first edition 1855 *Leaves of Grass* residing in a secret
   vault behind my bathroom vanity,
but rather, I think of dropping a lit match, of depositing a subtle
   cigarette butt in a pile of first drafts,
or of shooting an arrow of flame from Phoebus' bow and lighting
   the whole of it on fire. I think of sending
an offering of smoke and cinder, Romantics, Modernists, and neo-
   Formalists all equals in the eyes of ash.
That work done, a poetic holocaust worthy of Celan, I'd make my
   way out into the harsh light of the world.
Everything looks remarkably fresher, as it does after purging by
   great fire. A weight seems lifted.
The world has an aura, a corolla of gold, outlined in green.

Surgeon's Hands

Milton Bradley sure had it down, those kids' games of yesteryear,
        before XBox and more Playstations than you can count.
Remember *Operation*? The board with its anatomically incorrect,
        pear-shaped dolt with a nose that would light up
in cartoonish pain whenever your tiny metal forceps would touch
        the raw nerves surrounding such delicate human organs
as the funny bone, the wish bone, the breadbasket, or the Adam's
        apple? And that buzzer: the loud mechanical scream
of pain from the unanaesthetized patient. We played that game
        near to death. So much so, my mother had my father
crack open the housing and perform a buzzerectomy to protect her
        "very last nerve," which was not made of metal.
I remember the TV commercial: "It takes a very steady hand . . .
        BZZZZZ!!!" I wish the game had been what I made it:
putting the pieces back in that never needed removal in the first
        place. They always seemed benign to me.
Dropped from above by an oh, so steady hand, those pieces soothe
        our cold and hard interiors, they fill in our holes:
our funny bones, our wish bones, our breadbaskets, the Adam's
        apples of our eyes.

Results May Vary

So they said that last night on the T.V. You know, on one of those
        drug commercials,
not *those* kind of drugs, but medication. You know, the
        commercials where there is a middle age couple
or a whole family frolicking in a field or wrestling playfully
        in a backyard with a dog. You are never told
what, exactly, the drug is for. The voiceover, very confident
        and trustworthy, simply tells you to ask your doctor:
but if I did, and the drug was for, say, incontinence,
        which I certainly don't have,
or diabetes, which I don't think I have, or high cholesterol
        which I hope I don't have,
or that disease which I can't remember what it is called,
        but the one, you know, where you forget things,
which I'm pretty sure I don't have, mightn't my doctor laugh
        at me? Mightn't he say, "Oh, that.
You don't need that. You haven't got what that cures."
        But how could he be sure
since the commercial always has those three little words on the
        bottom of the screen: results may vary.
That seems, you know, when you really think about it, unsettling.
        I mean, if the results really vary,
it might not fix what ails you. It might make matters worse.
        It might fix something else. It might not make you feel
like that middle age couple or that family frolicking with the dog.
        You never know until you actually take it.
But what if I don't want to feel like them anyway, what if I want
        to feel like a biker or a trapeze artist or a
confirmed bachelor who has a llama? You don't, you know, frolic
        with a llama. It simply isn't done.
Maybe you just wait for a different commercial, or maybe, maybe
        it doesn't matter which pill you take: results may vary.

Bystander

It was, when you get right down to it, a rather nasty
accident. I was there, true, scratching something in my beard,
    but it was pure coincidence that had me stand-
ing just there. Tires squealed nearby as the tread
    desperately fought to cling, to snare
the road. No question but that they yearn-
    ed for traction as they left their black rubber brand
in double arcs along the road, the curb, then sidewalk, ready
    to take flight past the bridge, fitting just through the entry
provided by the break in the fence. The car strayed
    through that single gap in that line: between a bloom of aster
and the concrete piling. Struck dumb, what could I do but stare?
    I felt sure that no matter what, that vehicle was not rated
for such an event. For a moment, hand to my breast,
    I could feel nothing: no pump, no beat, the rhythm tardy.
I could only see where the car *had* been: bubbles, like yeast,
    rising to the surface, ripples from the impact washing the sand.
I thought then of the likelihood of some kind of beast
    of the deep seeing what I had seen, only inverted, with its beady
eye: How unusual, it thinks, snapping up a fish, sated.

Long Slow Fade

This is how they say it happens: first to go is the sound of the
voice:
        a breeze in leaves, the murmur

you strain your ears to hear: what was the pitch, the timbre, the
tone?
        Was the laugh a twinkle or a rumble?

Next, they say, fades the face: the lines and wrinkles from squinted
eyes
        and furrowed brow, then details

of eyelashes, nose, lower lip; are there teeth in the smile? Slowly,
like this,
        we evaporate from each other

until there is only the hazy outline of form, some vague mist of
color, and
        our own voices become each other's in our heads.

What we are left with are the days we have had and the way those
days have changed us:
        made us weep with laughter,

clench our fists in tiny balls, whiten our knuckles, pierce our hearts,
mend them again.
        What remains, then, all we are left with,

are those things nearest to us. Those things we could never forget.
Those things
        we could never see in the first place.

Reunion

Nights in the water, all those years ago: early Septembers,
        late Mays, tanned bodies surfacing in moonlight,
slick hair, eyes squinching salt, sidelong glances at flesh tightened
        by the chill of late or early season waters.
How many times we dove and rose and dove again to rise with
        someone new. Clinging together, buoying each other,
skin sliding on skin, the thinnest veneer of wide sea between us.
        How different now: how coarse the sand,
how it does get into places unwanted, how cold the sea in which
        we hold each other, interlocking gooseflesh for warmth
enough to pull us back into vaguely familiar harbors. It is not, we
        come to find, how long we have been swimming
that matters, but how far. Not the years, but the miles. For it
        comes to this: tonight we have brought towels.
And as we sit, cocooned in terry, we wave wistfully to our careless
        nights and breathe them a whispered *bon voyage*.

Tree of Knowledge

"Who told you that you were naked?" Always made me smile,
        that one. What a provocative choice: not
"Who told you that you were a brunette?" or, "Who told you that
        you were short?" No. He went with the naked one.
 Cut right to the chase, to the heart of all our present day concerns.
        I like to think about what might have been
if we hadn't eaten that apple: life would be just a little bit sweeter,
        wouldn't it? I mean, you'd have had
a shitty day at the office, lost a client or forgotten to file something
        important, and you'd gotten your ass chewed out
by the boss—much easier since there are now no pants covering
        it—but on your walk home, BAM!
Beautiful, nude woman: Long legs barely whispering together
        above the knee and at mid-calf, flat belly
with one of those rings in the navel, maybe the kind
        with the little dangly thingies jingling from it, and,
of course, breasts. Naked breasts. Perk you right up.
        Or you're in the supermarket, kids screaming
for a new ridiculous breakfast cereal and there, on aisle 9,
        looking at the brands of canned tomatoes,
is a young man straight out of an early-Sunday-morning-
        home-gym-infomercial—
all buffed and ripped, chest and shoulders slightly shiny in the
        fluorescent lighting, abs *pulsing*, and the kids just fade away.
You wouldn't be sure what to call this feeling, since we wouldn't
        know, well, *anything*, I suppose, but I'm sure you'd know
that you liked it. And you wouldn't be at all embarrassed
        if you were the day-making nymph or stud,
or even if you were thicker, or hairier, or saggier, or smaller—
        you wouldn't know that either. And if that were the case,
think how hard it would be to humiliate someone? No more
        picking on the fat kid. No more teenagers
hating themselves into their 30s, or 40s, or 50s. No more torture.
        No more secrets. There'd be nothing to know
in the first place, and nowhere to hide it if there were.

Channeling Cassandra

It's not like it was. We don't hear and disbelieve or misunderstand
        or simply look puzzled.
Now we just won't hear at all. She has too many others to
        compete with between network and cable—
we don't recognize her face: her curse is no longer unbelievability
        but anonymity: all we see are seers.
Standing in the crowd her too-weak voice adds only to the
        cacophony of her specious sisters.
At least when times were simpler, when we Trojans could *see* their
        Greek faces, when Helen walked the ramparts
and Paris could feel her in bed, at least then we *heard* if we didn't
        listen. At least we laughed or looked
obliquely, cast her a glance with raised eyebrows. At least we
        dismissed her. Now, rendered invisible and mute,
she pushes her chair back from the desk and unclips her
        microphone, her throat aches and
she lowers her eyes from the heavens, knowing her vision is
        all too true: armed with remotes
and our strong right thumbs, we will change her channels
        in midsentence.

Sleeping With the Seer

You are desperately trying to remember a dream;
        good fortune takes preparation.
Remember tomorrow is now, but live in the past:
        you have a reputation
for being deceitful and treacherous and believe foolishly in the
        goodness of mankind.
Nothing is as easy as it looks so the trouble with doing something
        right the first time is that
nobody appreciates how difficult it was:
        If at first you don't succeed, skydiving is not for you.
When the two of you are apart, you crave your lover;
        right now, thinking of you, is someone special.
To this popular idea be receptive. In the process of teaching
        someone something, you learn about another person,
such as that he has little understanding of the arts and music
        or that she has an evil heart and is much discussed.
Of all the things you wear, a smile is most important:
        tomorrow will be worse. You have a strong and sensitive
nose, to start trusting it is the smart thing to do:
        take shortcuts, avoid proven methods:
aggressively pursue your wishes: romance comes into your life
        in a very unusual way. Now is a good time
for an automobile servicing. Your lucky numbers are all positive
        integers < 100. These facts, though interesting,
are totally irrelevant. Your happiness is intertwined with
        your outlook on life: nice and soft words indicate
a weak cause; you work best on your own now.
        Keep to yourself—friendliness may make enemies.
There is only one happiness in life. A conclusion is the place
        where you tired of thinking. You are heading
for a land of darkness; perhaps you should go back to bed.

III

Later

What Wakes Us

In a dream, the graveyard burns. Each leaf an ember, red, edged in yellow. There, on the hill, three trees stand, sentinel fires, above the graves. Papery flames drift on the air, settling on the headstones, piling around their bases. Among the graves, one lies empty. The sod cut neatly away, the piled dirt beneath a green tarp. What remains is the bare patch of brown earth, a yawning, square-edged hole. Walking, a man might pause here, behind one of the larger monuments, shielded from the view of the mourners gathering slowly at the graveside. He might, then, see one flaming leaf drift, caught on the breeze, and disappear into the hole, disappear into the dark.

Untitled #4

Now here, in this place, one might be beautiful. Here, where a fresh wind brings scent of sea, of salt, and of you. Ripples the grass as your skin would—goosebumps at my touch, a gasp from you swiftly inhaled as lips and tongues and teeth meet. The crush of the mouth, the weight of legs and hair amid soft needles of fir. The sea pulses in time to the moon and a quickening of the blood. How fast this world spins—as quickly as the hearts we cling to—as we desperately try not to be thrown off.

View of the Marketplace

This would have been, as near as I can tell, about where my small table would have stood, next to the window, overlooking the marketplace where the vendors would haggle with grandmothers or where the fruit sellers would slip a fig or dried apricot into the hand of a child and wink. I would have been on the third floor, looking down, aroma of roasting almonds drifting upward. Now, I lean against what remains of the crumbling wall. I see the bus that carries mothers and children from the settlements splinter into fiery shrapnel. I hear the voices of the merchants gone startlingly silent. From underfoot I choose a scrap of paper that might have been from yesterday's news, or from the news of the day before that, and on it I begin to write a description of the torso of the child's doll I had kicked carelessly upon entering: fleshy pink garish against blackish char.

Still Life

In the still life of which I'm thinking, the one I never will paint, there are, of course, some exotic fruits, including, but not limited to, horned melon and lychee. There is a wadded-up grocery receipt upon which the only legible entry is "pineapple. . . . . 2.69" but no pineapple appears in the painting. There is a spool of thread, which may be black or navy blue depending upon the angle of the light and the viewer. There is no needle present for I threw it in the trash. Later, the men will come to haul the garbage away and will heft the bags in a giant hug, though I am quite sure they have been instructed against such handling. The needle will pierce a forearm or bicep, and a spot of blood will stain the shirtsleeve. Lastly, there is a small mirror, angled, to reflect a corner of the room. Visible in it is a dress mannequin covered in taupe fabric, and a large, elaborately wrought birdcage. Its tiny trapeze swings gently, its gilt door squeaks on its tiny hinge. In the corner, if one peers closely enough, a brief blur of yellow streaked with green.

Diner

The world doesn't stretch before us, it sits right here, in this diner. It is a couple in a booth, waiting for the meal, or, no, more likely, they've finished, and they loiter among the ruins of plates and half-empty coffee cups. She doodles his face on the placemat, beneath it writes a song lyric from what is playing on the small jukebox affixed to the booth's wall. "If anyone has ever had a heart." He tries to balance the salt shaker, angled, on a small pile of salt that he has spilled out upon the table. "I can never get this quite right," he says, to no one in particular. She looks up, studies his face, adds heavy shading somewhere on her placemat. "Neither can I."

Residue

Love me the way that the bees love the flowers. Flying from one to another, they stop to dust their legs with the honeying pollen. Let me dust your legs, so smooth and white, like candles, dripped from the hem of your skirt. Gather from me all that you can carry; perhaps next spring you will return for more of the soft grains, the yellow powder of love. Bathing, you will try to scrub the residue, but I shall cling, fine and thick and feathery—with the faint smell of disturbed dust in air and the rich feel of overturned soil.

Tomorrow, Tonight

Tomorrow, my heart starts beating. Tomorrow, my life can continue from the first pulse to the last, the first care to the last, from my first task to the final one. Tomorrow, let the business of the world and of living and breathing commence. But not tonight. Not this night. Let this night, of all nights, be the one when the earth ceases spinning. Let the moon hover where she is. Let this be the first night with you, my wonder, with you, my lovely one. Let the night hold and our love linger. Let the morning come as it must and with it day as it should. But not just yet.

Yard Work

And so we go about the business of shoveling snow. Labor that has piled up from the night before. With damp toes, cramped hands, aching backs, and frozen noses, we stand together removing the gift the plow has left at the foot of our drive, its pre-dawn effort to help everyone travel but allow no one leave. Silent but for the scrape of metal on macadam, we recall being out here months previous, when it was the barrage of leaves—salvos of windblown color—that kept us together. Before that, the garden, the flowers, the lawn. Tonight, again, the snow will rise to our waists, and drift, silently, over our heads.

Ride

When you look through the window and see past the condensation, built up like the way frost does when you wake up in the morning, you see the country around like the land, the buildings, the people and objects, the heart slums, the livestock and the farm equipment as you move down the road getting nauseated as the bus motors along, not so much because of the ride, but because your life is in some linear motion to some destination, yet you are still, and worse, not driving, so there is no break for coffee, or sights, or pees, at least not until the ride ends, but along the way there are the white pickups that pass you by with an ashtray full of cigarette butts and an 8track cassette that plays a hybrid of Johnny Cash and white noise as the driver howls along with a chainsaw in the bed and a shotgun in the rear window and a bumper sticker reading "if at first you don't secede, try, try again" and over there the mowed out swath of almond-colored grass where the grid towers of the power lines stretch for miles through the country ending at some transformer house somewhere in some state sending luminous screens of television to the trailers and shacks and farmhouses up and down route 29 and over there a plume of white against the graying sky of the day and with your forehead pressed against the glass, you dream you can smell the birch woodsmoke, but as you near, the white steadily becomes black as the leaves and grass have used engine oil and bald tires and the old dead dog piled on them as they burn while inside, Sarah cries into her pillow now that Skippy or Lucky or Sparky is dead while over there cows stand in Shell Mackey's spent yard with their hooves stained brown and bloodred from the clay mud they have turned up in their quest for graze as well as the cowpats that litter his fields in a connectthedots game of shit and waste that just slides into the stagnant pool where they drink their water: the cows and the Mackeys both, which is why Millie lays with fever now in a kerosenebright back room as her brothers watch dumbly, but there, outside Earls machine shop, farm equipment stands red and green and yellow and silent, rusting quietly under the drizzle of the four o'clock sky: that awkward light that fills in for day and takes over for the few hours before night and all of this you see before you have to wipe the moist from the window to see that next door there are the perfect fields of winter wheat with their deep, deep green, emerald, against the gray sky that goes from horizon to ceiling with no break and there sits the greenness juxtaposed with the next field which has gone fallow: a harsh saffron color of non-growth: that, split by the drive to Sunshade Farm: some rundown split level with an aged white fence surrounding its borders—its paint peeled and lead seeping to the ground defiling the leftover snow and right there are Ed Shifflet's cows starving this early in the winter because Ed's Donny ran off with that tramp and left Ed with no baled hay and the cows grazed the last of the land last week and one died yesterday, all because Donny ain't no good, like Ed's credit, but no one uses credit up there to the left at the Johnson Motel where a pink neon arrow blinks on and off and your eyelids follow in stride until you see the fat middle-age middle-management guy walk into room 27 that cost 37.50 with the high school girl that cost 75, but suddenly the driver turns off onto 230 and the windy road reminds you again that you aren't driving as you gaze at the lowlands near the creekbed all overflooded and swampy from the snow that melted from the rains that fell and swelled the creek into a river and you can see the pissshit yellowbrown waters flow in a rage over to where its cut a new oxbow and there, mingled with the roots of a toppled tree, is a cow, bloated and milkwhite, staring with eyes gnawed at by the crows: it lies there dead from struggling with the swelling water as it surges downstream to wherever this creek-turned-river surges to along the way watering the bare copse of beech trees that stand mute and lonely over the creek and the plain and the hills as they prick the gray where it pokes through the mountains—the mountains, hidden by a fog that makes them look like hills when really they tower into the air replete with whiskeystills and potfields and shotguns and rebelflags and a rolled over, rusted out, sky blue chevy a hundred yards or so up the mountain that looks like a 57, 58 maybe, but you don't see how it could have gotten there since from the road, it would've had to cross the creek bed and then up the slope that's too steep, otherwise, it'd have to roll down from the top but there's no road up to the top, though, so it looks just like some toy a child placed there and left behind like so many kids do with their toys—left it there rusting into the hill, but in a bit the driver will pull into the station and you will get out but you wont see your wife until you stand up from retrieving your bag and she waves solemnly and you follow her to the car, massaging your back where an errant and unruly spring lodged itself during the trip and you'll sit in the passenger seat in silence and enter the house in silence and you'll fix a bourbon while she fixes dinner in silence and in silence you'll go upstairs to the bedroom to unpack and unwind and while you hang your shirts and belts in the closet you'll see in the mirror why your wife is silent—she saw the long red hairs on your white shirt and smelled the pink perfume on your black jacket and you'll realize then, too, why you were silent—she is leaving now and you wont have to explain anything to her, especially not after the day you've had.

Heartbroken

From the wooded waterline, there, where I could not enter, a black winged heron emerged from the ether. I saw it pick through the brake and dip its curved thorn again and again into the murky broth. I watched, but it had taken nothing. Not even a token fish. I should like to offer it my heart, let this feathery thing peck at its pang and throb; let it be eaten. But I will not. Though I may be broken, let it be known: I am no hater of the things of this earth. I shall merely let them pass; allow them wide berth.

Matthew 14: 25-33

Along the Mill Valley Road, black treetops scrape late afternoon
sky, arthritic fingers stretch beyond their confines, scratch the
leaden ceiling above. Down the hill, the reservoir, and at its center,
a flock of gulls, dirty-robed in white and black. It would not be the
gulls themselves that might make one stop along that road, make
one pull over to that precarious sideslope of the narrowed
shoulder. What might make one pause is the sight of the gulls
walking on the water, standing up to their pale yellow mid-legs in
the thick and pearly meltwater just above the iceline. There, a flock
of scavenger messiahs, squawking and cackling amongst
themselves. Watching them, one might say, "Save me." Might say,
"if it is you, command me to come to you on the waters."

Pre-Fab

For a long time there was just the hole in the ground: backhoed and edged waiting for the shoring up by concrete. They poured the foundation when no one was looking and suddenly it happened. All those parts: walls and staircases, eaves and cupola, were ordered, built, delivered, laid out on the ground, then craned into place. All perfectly set and joined while the crew of men held their breath. They built a house that had been built already: constructed and taken apart, trucked, and put back together. Its twin stands next door, twenty yards distant, erected, it would seem, in the dead of night, sprung from another hole that had stood empty for so long. Some day, two different families will live side by side, in these identical houses. Some night, returning from afar, sleepy at the wheel, will one of them return home to the wrong drive, climb the stairs and walk the nineteen steps it takes to fall into a bed that doesn't feel quite right? A thinner blanket, a thicker pillow, a different view of that similar ceiling.

Winter Beach

Here, at the edge of the world, all that breaks the seamless gray is a thin line: the palest of yellows. It is all that separates the oncoming front from the outgoing tide. There is a lifeguard chair, its thin metal legs rusting into the sand, its wooden bench, warped and splintered. It stands mute watch over the leaden sea, the steel sky. This time of year a man might climb into that seat. He might clench each cold armrest and watch the armies of surf and sky amassed before him. He might, then, place all of his hopes in that band of light floating upon the horizon, and wonder if it will be enough.

Landscape #17

Small boats creak in the harbor, with only a token strain at their mooring lines, dangling kelp and dulse and carrageen. A girl, young enough, still, to be mistaken for a boy, lies face down on the dock, naked to the waist. Sunlight comes and goes, and with it, shadows glide silently beneath her skin, along the muscles of her back. If she were weeping, gently, her tears soaking into the splintered boards, rough and weathered by sea and wind and sky, might enough of them drip slowly down to the barnacles, cool in the shade of the lee side of the pilings? Might her tidepool tears be enough to coax them from the shells she fingers, reading their messages like the Braille of the world? Her long hair, spilling over the cracked rubber coping edging the dock, floats lightly upon the tide, mirroring so many anemones below, extending their fragile arms, waving them to any passersby, saying, this is our native land. Saying, you will arrive soon.

ABOUT THE AUTHOR

E. K. Mortenson is the author of the chapbooks, *The Fifteenth Station* (Accents Publishing, 2012) and *Dreamer or the Dream* (Last Automat Press, 2010. His work also appears in both print and online journals as well as anthologies. He was the 2008 recipient of the Leslie Leeds Poetry Prize, the 2012 Accents Publishing Chapbook Award, and is an instructor in the MFA in Creative and Professional Writing program at Western Connecticut State University. He writes and teaches in Pennsylvania where he lives with his wife and two children.

www.ingramcontent.com/pod-product-compliance
Lightning Source LLC
Chambersburg PA
CBHW031006090426
42737CB00008B/706